URSA

Where You DARE Not Go

Startling Stay

SCARY HOTELS AND INNS

by
Natalie Lunis and Sarah Parvis

Minneapolis, Minnesota

Credits
Cover, © XiXinXing/Shutterstock, © Bjoern Wylezich/Shutterstock, © Sabrina Janelle Gordon/Shutterstock, and © Lyudmila2509/Shutterstock; 4–5, © Difydave/iStock, © THEPALMER/iStock and © Andrey_Kuzmin/Shutterstock; 6, © Yingna Cai/Shutterstock; 8, © National Trails Office/Wikimedia Commons; 9, © fergregory/Adobe Stock, and © Alisusha/Shutterstock; 10, © Kenneth C. Zirkel/Creative Commons Attribution-Share Alike 4.0 International; 11, © MARGRIT HIRSCH/Shutterstock; 12, © Kevin Koeppen Photography/iStock; 13, © Girardta/Wikimedia Commons and © Anneka/Shutterstock; 14, © Schoening/Alamy Stock Photo; 16, © J Erick Brazzan/Shutterstock; 17, © DavidEwingPhotography/Shutterstock; 18, © Ub34m78/Creative Commons Attribution-Share Alike 3.0 Unported; 20, © Ana/Adobe Stock; 21, © Discovod/Shutterstock and © Discovod/Shutterstock; 22, © benedek/iStock; 23, © New Mexico's Digital Collections/Wikimedia Commons; 24, © William A. Morgan/Shutterstock; 25, © Civil War Glass Negatives/Library of Congress; 26, © Smallbones/Creative Commons CC0 1.0 Universal Public Domain Dedication; 27, © alipko/Adobe Stock; 28, © raksyBH/iStock; 29, © Lukas Gojda/Shutterstock; 30, © Laura Zeid/eStock Photo and © Cayobo/Creative Commons Attribution 1.0 Generic; 32, © Spiritwolf-Photography/Shutterstock; 33, © umnola/Adobe Stock; 34, © Allen Creative / Steve Allen/Alamy Stock Photo; 35, © UgurTandogan/Shutterstock; 36, © Derwyn/iStock; 37, © Andrey Kiselev/Adobe Stock; 38, © Barna Tanko/Shutterstock; 39, © Dean Fikar/Shutterstock; 40, © Dave Porter/Alamy Stock Photo; 41, © Nastasic/iStock.

Bearport Publishing Company Product Development Team
President: Jen Jenson; Director of Product Development: Spencer Brinker; Managing Editor: Allison Juda; Associate Editor: Naomi Reich; Associate Editor: Tiana Tran; Art Director: Colin O'Dea; Designer: Kim Jones; Designer: Kayla Eggert; Product Development Assistant: Owen Hamlin

Statement on Usage of Generative Artificial Intelligence
Bearport Publishing remains committed to publishing high-quality nonfiction books. Therefore, we restrict the use of generative AI to ensure accuracy of all text and visual components pertaining to a book's subject. See BearportPublishing.com for details.

Library of Congress Cataloging-in-Publication Data is available at www.loc.gov or upon request from the publisher.

ISBN: 979-8-89232-076-4 (hardcover)
ISBN: 979-8-89232-608-7 (paperback)
ISBN: 979-8-89232-209-6 (ebook)

Copyright © 2025 Bearport Publishing Company. All rights reserved. No part of this publication may be reproduced in whole or in part, stored in any retrieval system, or transmitted in any form or by any means, electronic, mechanical, photocopying, recording, or otherwise, without written permission from the publisher.

For more information, write to Bearport Publishing, 5357 Penn Avenue South, Minneapolis, MN 55419.

Contents

A Restful Night? 4
Portrait of a Ghost 6
A Gambler with a Grudge 8
Home at Last 10
Who Was Kate Morgan? 12
Tap . . . Tap . . . Tap 14
The Gray Ghost 16
Ghosts of Gettysburg 18
Party on the 13th Floor 20
One Last Stop 22
A Hotel or a Hospital? 24
A Ghostly Welcome 26
The Ghost of Room 218 28
Robert the Doll 30
A Stranger at the Inn 32
The Lady with the Lantern 34
The Worst Wedding Day 36
Remember the Alamo! 38
Stairway to Death 40

A World of . . . Startling Stays 42
Glossary 44
Read More 46
Learn More Online 46
Index 47

A Restful Night?

For most people, a room at a hotel or inn is a restful place to stay. It becomes a home away from home during a vacation or while traveling. After a few days, guests usually check out and go back to where they came from. Some people, however, check in but never seem to check out!

The next time you stay in the room of a hotel or inn, beware. You may witness an eerie shadow or a glowing light. You could hear footsteps or moaning when no one is there. What if you aren't the only guest in the room . . . ?

Portrait of a Ghost

LONGFELLOW'S WAYSIDE INN
SUDBURY, MASSACHUSETTS

Longfellow's Wayside Inn is the oldest inn in America that is still open to guests. It was started in 1716 by David Howe and his wife, Hepzibah. Other members of the family ran the business until 1861. One of them, it seems, never left—even long after new owners took over.

Longfellow's Wayside Inn

Jerusha Howe was the great-granddaughter of the inn's first owners. Lively and talented, she often played the piano for guests. Sometime in the early 1800s, she fell in love with an Englishman. He sailed back to England, but he promised to return and marry her. Sadly, he was never heard from again. Jerusha was heartbroken. After his disappearance, she rarely left her room on the second floor. There she stayed until her death in 1842.

Since then, people claim that Jerusha has reappeared as a ghost, usually on the second floor. Guests have reported hearing unexplained footsteps and soft piano music. They have noticed the smell of a lemony perfume. Some visitors have felt a spirit touch them as they walked by. Others have heard whisperings in their ears.

One guest actually saw the inn's ghost so clearly that she was able to draw the spirit. Did the picture look just like the woman who had lived on the second floor more than 100 years ago? No one knows, because no drawings were made of Jerusha during her lifetime.

The inn is named for the poet Henry Wadsworth Longfellow. After staying at the inn in 1862, Longfellow wrote *Tales of a Wayside Inn* based on his visit. After the book was published, the inn's owner changed its name from Howe's Tavern to Longfellow's Wayside Inn.

A Gambler with a Grudge

ST. JAMES HOTEL, CIMARRON, NEW MEXICO

From the 1860s to the 1890s, New Mexico was part of America's Wild West. With few sheriffs and even fewer laws, it is no surprise that outlaws liked to live there. Many who were handy with a pistol stayed at the St. James Hotel, including Jesse James and Billy the Kid. While these dangerous gunslingers are now long dead, the ghost of one angry customer still makes trouble at the hotel.

St. James Hotel

In 1901, the owners of the St. James Hotel decided to replace its roof. Imagine their surprise when they found more than 400 bullet holes in the ceiling. This historic hotel had certainly had more than its share of gunfights—and murders.

One unlucky victim was the gambler Thomas James Wright. He was shot in the back after winning the hotel in a poker game. He dragged himself into room 18 and slowly bled to death.

Since then, Wright's angry spirit is said to shove anyone who sets foot in what he considers his room. So now, the hotel owners keep the haunted room locked. No guests are allowed to sleep where the man lay dying more than 100 years ago.

Every Halloween, the owners of the St. James Hotel pour a glass of whiskey for Wright's ghost and leave it in his room. The next morning, it is always gone.

Home at Last

JARED COFFIN HOUSE
NANTUCKET, MASSACHUSETTS

With its history of seafaring and whaling, it's no wonder that the Massachusetts island of Nantucket is said to be filled with ghosts. After all, many young sailors lost their lives at sea. One Nantucket sea captain, however, followed a different course. He lived a long life before coming back to haunt the house that he had built on the island.

Jared Coffin House

Jared Coffin was not only a sea captain but also a successful owner of whaling ships. As a result, in 1845 he was able to have a three-story brick mansion built for himself and his wife in the center of Nantucket. Within less than a year, however, the Coffins went off to live in Boston. Why? Some people say that Mrs. Coffin wanted to live in a big city. Others say she disliked the smell that came from a nearby building as it melted down whale blubber to make lamp oil and other products.

About a year after its owners left, the house survived a fire that burned down much of the town around it. The building was then bought and turned into an inn. According to those who know the place well, guests are not the only ones who enjoy its comforts. Often, when there is an empty rocking chair near a cozy fire, it rocks slowly back and forth. People say it isn't really empty, however. They think it's occupied by the spirit of Jared Coffin, back to enjoy his beautiful Nantucket home at last.

The Jared Coffin House survived the fire of 1846 because it was made of brick. The houses and buildings that burned were made of wood.

Who Was Kate Morgan?

HOTEL DEL CORONADO
CORONADO, CALIFORNIA

Kate Morgan checked into the Hotel del Coronado in November 1892. She was supposed to meet her husband there. Five days later, she was found dead on the stairs behind the hotel. Who killed her? Unless Kate's ghost starts talking, no one will ever know.

Hotel del Coronado

Kate Morgan and her husband, Tom, were gamblers. In the late 1880s they traveled around the country by train winning money in card games. By 1892, however, Kate had had enough. She told her husband that she wanted to stop their life of gambling. So she left Tom and checked into the Hotel del Coronado.

Kate Morgan

Tom had agreed to meet Kate at the hotel for Thanksgiving, but he never arrived. Kate was found shot in the head five days later. The police were sure she had killed herself. Others believed her husband sneaked into town and murdered her.

Since Kate's death, strange things have happened in the room where she stayed. Guests have heard voices when no one else is around. Some have seen curtains move when there is no breeze. Others have even spotted the ghost of a woman staring out the window, as if waiting for someone. Perhaps Kate has never left, still hoping Tom will arrive.

The light over the steps where Kate's body was found will not stay lit. When the bulb is replaced, it quickly burns out again.

Tap... Tap... Tap

THE GREEN MOUNTAIN INN
STOWE, VERMONT

People say when ghosts are present in a home or an inn, it's because they are the spirits of people who were born or died there. Or perhaps they spent an especially important part of their lives in the building. All of these facts are true in the case of Boots Berry, whose ghost has haunted a Vermont inn since the 1800s.

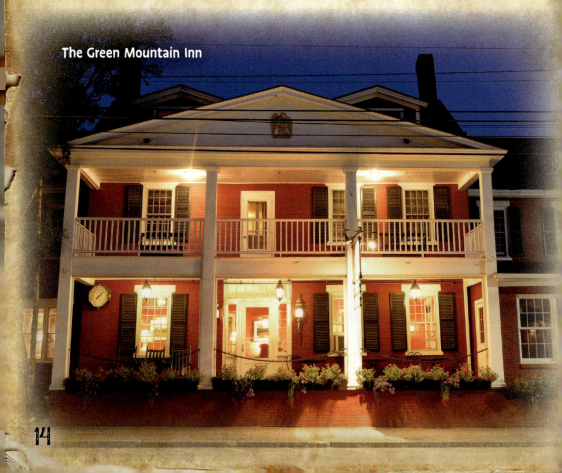

The Green Mountain Inn

Boots Berry lived a life that was full of ups and downs. In 1840, the year he was born, his mother worked as a maid at the Green Mountain Inn, and his father worked as a horseman. Boots grew up at the inn. In time, he became a horseman as well. He also became a hometown hero one day when he stopped the horses pulling a runaway stagecoach and saved the lives of the passengers inside.

Sadly, the Vermont man's life took a downward turn after that. He started drinking too much and was fired from his job. He then wandered near and far, ending up in jail in New Orleans. It was there that he got his nickname, Boots, when a fellow prisoner taught him to tap-dance.

After a while, Boots returned to Vermont and the inn. There, he again saved a life when a little girl became trapped on the roof during a snowstorm. Boots helped her back to safety but then slipped and fell off the roof to his death. Since that time, on cold, stormy nights, people inside the inn say they have heard the sound of tapping.

Boots was born on the inn's third floor in Room 302. People say that when he slipped off the roof, he fell past the window of this room. Today, Room 302 is where Boots's tapping can be heard the loudest.

The Gray Ghost

QUEEN MARY FLOATING HOTEL
PORT OF LONG BEACH, CALIFORNIA

The *Queen Mary* first set sail in 1936. This fancy ocean liner was bigger, faster, and more powerful than the *Titanic*. It crossed the Atlantic Ocean more than 1,000 times. During World War II (1939-1945), the ship was painted gray and used by the military. Nicknamed The Gray Ghost, it carried more than 800,000 soldiers over the years. The ship's speed and size helped save thousands of soldiers. Unfortunately, they killed some, too.

The *Queen Mary*

In October 1942, the *Queen Mary* and the H.M.S. *Curacao* were traveling together. To avoid enemy torpedoes, the two ships zigzagged in the ocean. When the *Curacao* mistakenly turned into the other ship's path, the *Queen Mary* sliced the smaller ship in half. The *Curacao* sank quickly. About 330 men died before help arrived.

In 1967, the *Queen Mary* stopped making trips. The boat was permanently docked in Long Beach, California, and was turned into a hotel. The ghosts of the *Curacao's* doomed sailors, however, still haunt the ship. Members of the hotel staff have heard the sound of rushing water and banging noises near the part of the *Queen Mary* that hit the *Curacao*. Some even claim to hear the screams of the *Curacao's* dying crew echoing throughout the hotel.

The sinking of the *Curacao* was not the only deadly accident caused by the *Queen Mary*. On July 10, 1966, John Pedder, an 18-year-old crew member, was crushed to death by one of the ship's heavy doors. His ghost has since been seen near the engine room.

Ghosts of Gettysburg

FARNSWORTH HOUSE INN
GETTYSBURG, PENNSYLVANIA

Guests at this Pennsylvania inn claim that the ghost of a boy plays tricks on visitors in one of the rooms. The spirit of a man who is thought to be his father has been heard pacing nervously in the hall outside. That's only a small part of the inn's ghostly activity, however. After all, the building is located in the heart of Gettysburg—a place where thousands died in one of the bloodiest battles of the U.S. Civil War (1861–1865).

Farnsworth House Inn

The 200-year-old building now known as the Farnsworth House Inn started taking in paying guests around 1900. Not long after, people say, a terrible accident occurred there. A young boy ran out into the street and was hit by a horse-drawn carriage. He was brought indoors while a doctor was called, but it was too late. The boy died while his father waited and worried. Today, some people believe that both the young boy and his father have remained at the inn as ghosts.

Their spirits are far from alone. About 40 years before the boy's death, from July 1 to July 3, 1863, around 165,000 Civil War soldiers from the North and South fought one another in and around Gettysburg. During the three-day battle, a group of Southern sharpshooters entered the building, which was still a private home at the time. They stationed themselves at windows in the attic and in other rooms. By the end of the 3 days, the sharpshooters were killed, along with about 7,000 other soldiers from both sides. The presence of the Southern soldiers is still sensed by visitors to the Farnsworth House Inn, especially in the form of voices and footsteps—all coming from the attic.

Today, much of Gettysburg is said to be haunted by the spirits of Civil War soldiers who died there. Many people say that a fog with horses and riders moving inside it sometimes appears on the former battlefield at night.

Party on the 13th Floor

BILTMORE HOTEL, CORAL GABLES, FLORIDA

The Biltmore Hotel was built for $10 million in 1926. It was opened during Prohibition, a time when it was illegal to make or sell alcohol in the United States. Yet that didn't stop the Biltmore. The 13th floor of the hotel was home to a speakeasy. It also had a casino. A number of gangsters went there to drink and gamble. It seems one of them has stuck around for a good time.

Biltmore Hotel

Thomas "Fatty" Walsh was a Florida gangster. He worked with many criminals and he made a lot of enemies. In 1929, he was shot and killed on the 13th floor of the Biltmore Hotel.

Even in death, however, Fatty seems to want to keep the party going at the Biltmore. According to some guests, the lights in the hotel's elevator suddenly turn on and off. The elevator sometimes passes the guests' floor and goes straight to the 13th floor.

One woman who was taken to the empty floor said she smelled cigars burning. She called out, but no one answered. She heard the sound of laughter, even though no one was there. Somehow, the party never ends for Thomas "Fatty" Walsh—the ghostly gangster.

One guest riding in the Biltmore's elevator made the mistake of saying that Fatty got what he deserved. The elevator suddenly screeched to a stop. Someone suggested she apologize. Once she did, the elevator continued its ride.

One Last Stop

LA FONDA ON THE PLAZA
SANTA FE, NEW MEXICO

The hotel that now stands on the Plaza in Santa Fe has been around since 1922. However, there has been some kind of inn or hotel at this spot for 400 years, going all the way back to the days when New Mexico was a Spanish colony. Since then, many ghosts are said to have gathered at the busy spot in the center of town—including one who can't stop repeating his last day on Earth.

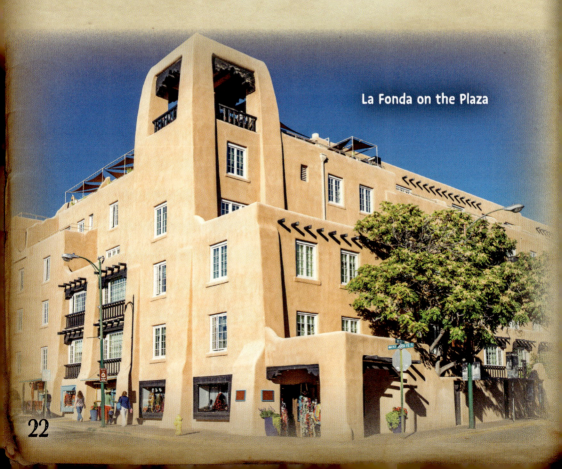

La Fonda on the Plaza

During the 1800s, Santa Fe's downtown area became busier than ever. That's because in 1821, the Santa Fe Trail was opened. The 900-mile-long (1,400 km) route connected the capital of New Mexico to Franklin, Missouri. It provided a path for pioneers, cowboys, and traders through the American West.

The Santa Fe Trail

By the 1860s, thousands of people were traveling and doing business along the Trail. One of them was a salesman who stopped at Santa Fe's Plaza and spent time at a popular gambling hall that belonged to the hotel. Not being very lucky, however, the man lost all his company's money. As soon as he realized what he had done, he jumped to his death down a deep well that was just outside the hall.

The restaurant at today's La Fonda on the Plaza is built over the spot where that well once stood. According to diners and staff members, the ghost of the salesman sometimes makes a shocking appearance. Even more shocking is the way the ghost disappears—by jumping into the floor and down an unseen well that lies beneath.

La fonda means inn in Spanish.

A Hotel or a Hospital?

HOTEL PROVINCIAL
NEW ORLEANS, LOUISIANA

During the Civil War, there were not enough hospitals to take care of all the sick and injured soldiers. So, other buildings had to be used as well. The Hotel Provincial was turned into one of these temporary hospitals. While the building is now a hotel again, some say its patients have never left.

Hotel Provincial

Building number 5 is reported to be the spookiest section of the Hotel Provincial. Once, a hotel worker watched an entire scene from the past brought back to life there. As the elevator doors opened, he did not see the regular hallway. Instead, the bodies of bloody Civil War soldiers covered the floor. They moaned and cried out for help, as if the Provincial were still their hospital.

Staff members aren't the only ones seeing strange spirits from the past. Guests have seen the ghosts of Civil War soldiers and doctors roaming the halls. Some sad souls reach out as if they need an arm to lean on. One guest stepped out of the shower and saw what looked like a pile of towels on the floor. Looking closer, she realized that they were bloody bandages and sheets. When she tried to pick them up, they disappeared.

Wounded Civil War soldiers outside a temporary hospital

People have reported seeing bloodstains mysteriously appear and disappear on the beds in some rooms at the Hotel Provincial.

A Ghostly Welcome

THE QUEEN ANNE HOTEL
SAN FRANCISCO, CALIFORNIA

The building that now serves as the Queen Anne Hotel was not always a place for travelers and other overnight guests to stay. When it was built in 1890, it served as Miss Mary Lake's School for Girls. Mary Lake, the headmistress, showed great kindness and helpfulness as a teacher. Many people think she continues to show these qualities as she haunts the place she once loved.

The Queen Anne Hotel

Unfortunately, Miss Mary Lake's School closed after only six years, probably because there was not enough money to keep the expensive boarding school running. For the next 40 years, the elegant pink building that had housed the school was used by different groups. Then, for the next 50, it mostly stood empty and rundown. Finally, during the 1980s, it was restored inside and out to its former beauty and reopened as the Queen Anne Hotel.

Many guests and workers believe that the hotel's appearance is not the only thing that goes back to the building's early days. They're also convinced that Mary Lake has returned to the inn's rooms and hallways. What makes them think so? Mary's reflection has often been seen in a hall mirror and a misty figure is sometimes spotted there. Even more mysterious, in certain rooms, bags have been unpacked and clothing has been hung up when no one was around. One guest was even tucked in during a nap. It seems that after a long time of being away, Mary is happy to once again show her caring nature.

People say that Mary is most active in Suite 410—a room with a fireplace and an extra sitting area that was once her office at the school.

The Ghost of Room 218

THE CRESCENT HOTEL
EUREKA SPRINGS, ARKANSAS

In the late 1800s, many people believed that the water from Eureka Springs could cure their diseases. People who were ill traveled there from all over the United States, hoping to get better. Many of them stayed at the Crescent Hotel—a building that has been haunted since the time it was built.

The Crescent Hotel

Construction began on the Crescent Hotel in 1884. Within a year, it had its first ghostly guest. In 1885, a worker named Michael lost his balance and fell from the roof. He died in the area of the building that became room 218. It is said that his ghost plays tricks there.

Guests complain that Michael's ghost shakes them awake at night and slams doors. He pounds on the walls and turns the television on and off. The wife of one of the hotel's owners tried sleeping in room 218 and did not make it through the night. She came running out after seeing what looked like blood splashed all over the walls. Maybe she was dreaming. Or maybe Michael was just playing another ghostly prank in room 218.

During the early 1900s, the Crescent Hotel was home to a women's college. The death of one of its students remains a mystery. Did she fall or was she pushed from the fourth-floor deck? Her sad spirit is often seen in the beautiful hotel gardens.

Robert the Doll

THE ARTIST HOUSE, KEY WEST, FLORIDA

Many inns and small hotels were once private homes. That's true of the Artist House. The beautiful Florida mansion was once the home of a famous painter. It was also the home of a very strange doll named Robert, who seems to have had a mind of its own.

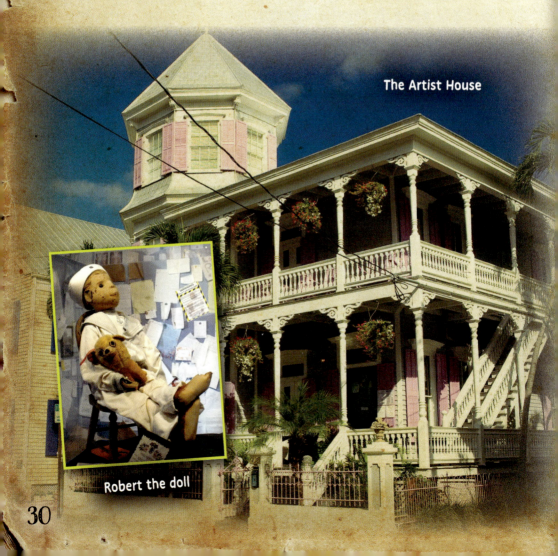

The Artist House

Robert the doll

The inn now known as the Artist House was built in the late 1890s by Thomas Otto and his wife, Minnie. In 1898, their four-year-old son, Robert Eugene Otto, received a cloth doll as a gift. The doll looked like a life-size boy and wore a sailor suit. Its young owner, who was known as Gene, gave the doll his own first name, Robert.

Before long, people started noticing strange things about Robert, such as changes in the doll's expression. Children on the street said they saw the doll move while it sat by an attic window. Sometimes, the sound of giggling came from the top floor when Robert was up there alone.

During the 1920s, Gene left home to study painting in New York and Paris. Later, he returned to the house where he had grown up, bringing his new wife, Anne, with him. According to reports, the couple found Robert there, and the strange events began occurring all over again. After Gene's death, the house became a hotel. What happened to Robert? By that time he was famous in Key West, and so he was given to a small museum in town. Reportedly, he continues to cause mischief there.

It is said that visitors to the museum must ask Robert's permission before taking a photo—otherwise the doll will put a curse on them and bring them bad luck. The walls of the glass case where Robert is kept are covered with letters asking him to remove some of these curses.

A Stranger at the Inn

JAMAICA INN, CORNWALL, ENGLAND

The Jamaica Inn was built in 1750. Smugglers, highway robbers, and other criminals would often stop there. One of the inn's best-known ghosts is thought to have been killed by one of these troublemakers.

Jamaica Inn

Many years ago, a stranger entered the Jamaica Inn and ordered a drink. He may have been a sailor, a smuggler, or simply a tired traveler passing through. Shortly afterward, another man appeared. He and the stranger stepped outside. The mysterious stranger was never seen alive again. His dead body was found outside the next day.

Who was this stranger? No one knows for sure. Some say he still haunts the Jamaica Inn. People have reported seeing his ghost sitting on the stone wall outside the building. Many strange noises at the inn are thought to come from the ghost of the murdered stranger. Guests have heard footsteps where no one was walking. They have heard conversations in a language they couldn't understand. Is it the murdered stranger trying to let people know the truth about what happened years ago?

It has been a long time since people traveled by stagecoach. Some of the Jamaica Inn ghosts, however, still seem to travel that way. People have heard the sound of horses' hooves and the rattle of a carriage on cobblestones. Yet when they go outside, no one is there.

The Lady with the Lantern

CASABLANCA INN, ST. AUGUSTINE, FLORIDA

St. Augustine, Florida, is the oldest city in the United States. It also has the country's oldest port. Many stories from its past are filled with pirates and smugglers. One of the eeriest tells of a ghost that is still sending secret messages to ships from a waterfront inn.

Casablanca Inn

Casablanca Inn was built in 1914 on an old street with a good view of the water. During the 1920s, a local widow bought it and gave it its current name. At first, the inn was a success—always clean, comfortable, and filled with guests. After a while, however, its owner needed more money to keep the inn running. It was then that she started doing business with rum-runners.

Alcohol, including rum, was illegal during this period of Prohibition. Rum-runners, or people who transported and sold rum, needed to steer clear of government agents. To help them do so, the owner of the Casablanca Inn would send a warning if she knew the agents were in town. She would climb to the roof of the inn and swing a lantern. If the smugglers, who were traveling in boats, saw the light, they would keep going. Today, almost 100 years later, people in boats off the coast as well as visitors walking along the waterfront sometimes see a light swinging in the same spot—even though no one is there.

People in St. Augustine know the innkeeper's name but they usually call her simply the Lady with the Lantern. They keep her real name private out of respect for the rest of her family, because what she did was illegal.

The Worst Wedding Day

THE FAIRMONT BANFF SPRINGS HOTEL
BANFF, ALBERTA, CANADA

A wedding day is usually one of the happiest days of a person's life. For one woman at the Fairmont Banff Springs Hotel, this day was also her last. The ghost of this bride is still waiting to walk down the aisle.

The Fairmont Banff Springs Hotel

On her wedding day, the beautiful bride was dressed in a long white gown. The staircase at the Fairmont Banff Springs Hotel glowed with the light from many candles. As the bride made her way down the stairs, however, something went terribly wrong.

According to some stories, her dress touched a candle and caught fire. Terrified, she tried to put out the flames and began to tumble down the staircase. Other stories say the poor woman just tripped on her dress. Whatever the reason, the bride fell down the stairs and died.

Guests of the Fairmont Banff Springs Hotel have since reported spotting the ghostly bride wandering the halls. She has also been seen on the stairs where she took her tumble. Others have seen this sad ghost waltzing in the ballroom. Still in her beautiful gown, she finally gets to dance at her wedding.

The Fairmont Banff Springs Hotel is also home to a ghostly bellhop named Sam. He retired in 1967 and died a few years after that. Yet his spirit still helps out guests. He has been known to unlock doors for those who've lost their keys.

Remember the Alamo!

THE MENGER HOTEL, SAN ANTONIO, TEXAS

Over time, the Menger Hotel has become known not only as one of the finest places to stay in Texas but also one of the most haunted. Some of its ghosts are found within the historic building on Alamo Square. Others roam just outside.

The Menger Hotel

When it was first built in 1859, the Menger Hotel was no more than a small inn. Tired cowboys spent the night there before moving on. The place was so successful that its owner, William Menger, soon added on another building. Then, even more rooms were built. By the end of the 1800s, the Menger was drawing people not only from all over Texas but also from all around the world. Presidents Ulysses S. Grant and Theodore Roosevelt are a few of the famous people who stayed there.

According to some guests, the hotel has drawn many ghosts as well. Among those who have been spotted inside are Sallie White, a hotel maid who was murdered by her husband in 1876, and Richard King, a wealthy rancher who died in one of the rooms in 1885. Just outside the hotel is the Alamo—a fort where around 200 Texans died while fighting for independence from Mexico in 1836. Guests whose windows look out onto the Alamo claim to have seen ghosts of the battle wandering the grounds at night.

The Alamo

After the battle of the Alamo, the general in charge of the Mexican troops ordered his men to destroy the fort. According to legend, however, ghostly hands reached out to stop the men. The terrified soldiers fled, and the Alamo remained standing.

Stairway to Death

THE TALBOT HOTEL, OUNDLE, ENGLAND

More than 400 years ago, Mary, Queen of Scots was executed in an English castle. Yet today, she has been seen—in the form of a ghost—walking to her death down a stairway in a hotel that is about 3.5 miles (5.6 km) away. Why is she there?

The Talbot Hotel

In 1586, Mary Stuart, also known as Mary, Queen of Scots, was put on trial for plotting against her cousin Elizabeth, who was Queen of England. Mary was found guilty, and not long after, she was sentenced to be beheaded. Both the trial and the execution took place at Fotheringhay Castle in the central part of England.

Mary, Queen of Scots

About 50 years after Mary's death, the castle was abandoned and demolished. However, people from nearby towns took away the materials that had been used to build it. Windows, stones from its walls, and even a beautiful oak staircase were used to rebuild a very old tavern in the town of Oundle.

Today, that English tavern is a hotel known as the Talbot. Guests and workers there sometimes see a ghostly woman in a long dress on the staircase. Sometimes, she is gazing out the window at the top of the staircase. Other times, she starts coming down the stairs. Not surprisingly, people assume the ghost is Mary, retracing the steps she walked on the last day of her life.

People in the hotel have also heard sobbing coming from one of the rooms. However, when they checked, there was no one inside.

A World of...

Startling Stays

- A tap-dancing phantom in Stowe, Vermont
- A heartbroken spirit in Sudbury, Massachusetts
- Civil War ghosts in Gettysburg, Pennsylvania
- A restless whaler in Nantucket, Massachusetts
- An angry spirit in Eureka Springs, Arkansas
- A warning to rum-runners in St. Augustine, Florida
- A haunted elevator in Coral Gables, Florida
- Bloody bodies in New Orleans, Louisiana
- Alamo soldiers in San Antonio, Texas
- Robert the Doll in Key West, Florida

43

Glossary

beheaded put to death by having one's head chopped off

bellhop a person who works in a hotel carrying luggage and helping guests

blubber a layer of fat under the skin of whales

boarding school a school where students live and study

carriage a vehicle that has wheels, often pulled by horses

casino a room or building used for gambling

Civil War the war in the United States between the northern and southern states that lasted from 1861 until 1865

colony an area that has been settled by people from another country and is ruled by that country

curse something that brings or causes evil or misfortune

demolished destroyed

docked placed in the landing area where ships load and unload goods

eerie mysterious or strange

executed put to death

fort a strong building from which people can defend an area

gambling hall a place where people play cards and other games of chance to win money

gangsters people who are part of a group of criminals

grief great sadness

gunslingers people who are able to shoot a gun with great skill and speed

headmistress a female teacher who is in charge of a school

highway robbers criminals who steal from people traveling on country roads

horseman a person who takes care of horses

illegal against the law

inn a small hotel

legend a story handed down from the past that may be based on fact but is not always completely true

mansion a very large and grand house

military having to do with the armed forces

mischief playful behavior that may cause trouble

ocean liner a large ship that can carry many people or lots of goods

outlaws criminals who are running away from the law

pioneers people or groups that explore new areas

pistol a small gun

plaza a town square

port a place where ships load and unload goods

Prohibition the period of time in U.S. history, between 1920 and 1933, when the sale of alcohol was against the law

renovated improved the condition of something

retired stopped working forever, usually because of age

route the road a person follows to get from one place to another

seafaring going, traveling, or working on the sea

sharpshooters soldiers who fire on an enemy from a hidden spot or from a distance

smugglers people who secretly bring in or take out goods in a way that is against the law

speakeasy a place that illegally sells alcoholic drinks

spirit a supernatural creature, such as a ghost

stagecoach a carriage that is pulled by horses

tavern a place where people stop to eat and drink

temporary lasting for a short period of time; not permanent

well a deep hole dug in the ground to get water

whaling the hunting of whales from ships at sea

widow a woman whose husband has died

Read More

Hamilton, S. L. *The World's Most Ghoulish Ghosts (Xtreme Screams).* Minneapolis: ABDO Publishing Company, 2022.

Keppeler, Jill. *More Freaky Stories about the Paranormal (Freaky True Science).* New York: Gareth Stevens Publishing, 2020.

Morrison, Marie. *The Queen Mary Is Haunted! (Haunted History).* New York: PowerKids Press, 2020.

Snowden, Matilda & Joyce Markovics. *Investigating Ghosts in Hotels (Investigating Ghosts).* Hallandale Beach, FL: Mitchell Lane Publishers, 2021.

Learn More Online

1. Go to **www.factsurfer.com** or scan the QR code below.

2. Enter "**Startling Stay**" into the search box.

3. Click on the cover of this book to see a list of websites.

Index

Alamo, the 38-39, 43
Artist House, the 30-31
Battle of Gettysburg 18-19
Berry, Boots 14-15
Billy the Kid 8
Biltmore Hotel 20-21
Casablanca Inn 34-35
Civil War 18-19, 24-25, 43
Coffin, Jared 11
Crescent Hotel, the 28-29
Fairmont Banff Springs Hotel, the 36-37
Farnsworth House Inn 18-19
Fotheringhay Castle 41
Green Mountain Inn, the 14-15
H.M.S. *Curacao* 17
Hotel del Coronado 12-13
Hotel Provincial 24-25
Howe, Jerusha 7
Jamaica Inn 32-33
James, Jesse 8
Jared Coffin House 10-11
King, Richard 39
La Fonda on the Plaza 22-23
Lake, Mary 26-27
Longfellow, Henry Wadsworth 7
Longfellow's Wayside Inn 6-7
Mary, Queen of Scots 40-41
Menger Hotel, the 38-39

Morgan, Kate 12-13
Otto, Robert Eugene 31
Pedder, John 17
Prohibition 35
Queen Anne Hotel, the 26-27
Queen Mary 16-17
Robert the Doll 30-31, 43
Santa Fe Trail 23
St. James Hotel 8-9
Talbot Hotel, the 40-41
Walsh, Thomas "Fatty" 21
White, Sallie 39
World War II 16-17
Wright, Thomas James 9

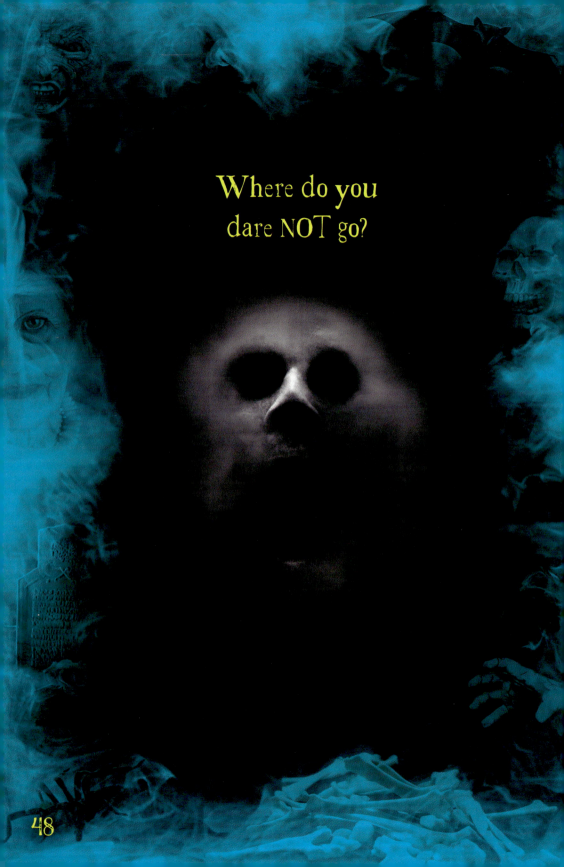